When the alarm bell rings the firemen have to put on their uniforms as quickly as possible, so they are hung, with boots and overtrousers standing ready, so that they can be donned with the minimum of delay. Here firemen in 1936 prepare to attend a call.

FIREMEN'S UNIFORM

Brian Wright

Shire Publications Ltd

CONTENTS

Printed in Great Britain by C. I. Thomas & Sons (Haverfordwest) Ltd, Press Buildings, Merlins Bridge, Haverfordwest, Dyfed SA61 1XF.

British Library Cataloguing in Publication Data: Wright, Brian, 1951-. Firemen's uniform. I. Title. 391.043633. ISBN 0-7478-0137-1.

ACKNOWLEDGEMENTS
The author wishes to thank all those who offered help in one form or another: Wing Commander Bruce Allcorn of RAF FSCTE, RAF Manston; Alan Dagnall; Kenneth Geering; the Guardian Royal Exchange Insurance Group; John Hallam; Sherre Leeds, for all her help in setting up the cover photograph; Russell MacLean; Ian McMurtrie, Curator of the Fire Museum, Lothian and Borders Fire Brigade; the Museum of Science and Engineering, Newcastle upon Tyne; Norfolk Fire Service and the men of Norwich Fire Brigade; Norwich Union Insurance Group; John Rodwell, Curator of the London Fire Brigade Museum; the Royal Insurance Group; Ian Scott; Brian Sharp; David Spracklan; Louisa Steel, Training Department, London Fire and Civil Defence Authority; David Trotter, for taking the cover photograph; Walsall Local History Centre, for permission to reproduce the photograph of Darlaston Fire Brigade; Elizabeth Wright; and last, but not least, Valerie Wright for once again reading a manuscript and making helpful suggestions.

Cover: *The old and the new. The working uniform of a fireman of the Norwich Union Insurance Company, c.1810, contrasts strongly with the uniform worn by a present-day member of the Norwich Fire Brigade. (The author is grateful to the Norwich Union Insurance Group and the Norfolk Fire Service for setting up this photograph.)*

Below: *An industrial fire brigade in 1989 at the handing over of a new fire appliance. All the firemen wear blue tunics, yellow overtrousers and yellow helmets. Two wear one-piece chemical protection suits, while the female firefighter (far left) wears a bib with a diced pattern showing she is responsible for recording the names and other details of firemen who enter a building wearing breathing apparatus. Two firemen are wearing breathing apparatus, while in the centre can be seen the Chief Fire Officer of the county.*

A fireman and porter (salvage man) of the Bristol Crown Fire Office are depicted on an early eighteenth-century insurance policy. The fireman wears a close-fitting buttoned tunic, collarless with a wide skirt. This is belted at the waist and worn with breeches and shoes. The porter is provided with a coarse spun apron and a rather shapeless hat.

COATS OF MANY COLOURS

Fighting fires is often hazardous work, and today's firefighters are provided with both a protective 'working uniform' and a second uniform for wear when engaged in other duties. Wearing a uniform creates a bond between the members of the brigade and both distinguishes them from other people and identifies them as firemen. It is not widely known just how long uniformed fire brigades have been in existence in Britain or how their uniform evolved.

Fires had always been a common occurrence, but between the Roman period and the mid seventeenth century there was little organised firefighting, and certainly no uniformed fire brigades existed. However, in 1680 Nicolas Barbon, in partnership with others, started the first fire insurance company, known simply as the Fire Office, and established a part-time fire brigade. At first the Fire Office had a monopoly of fire insurance, but in 1684 the Friendly Society was founded, and in 1696 the Amicable Contributionship (later known as the Hand in Hand Fire Office) was established. Both of these new enterprises had their own brigades, and the insurance companies of London and the provinces provided the main firefighting force during the eighteenth and early nineteenth centuries.

The London insurance companies drew their part-time firemen from the ranks of the Free Watermen who operated a 'water taxi' service on the river Thames. They were particularly suitable since they were self-employed, tough and generally reliable. Uniforms were brightly coloured, red, green, blue, brown and so on, to distinguish the various fire brigades. To modern eyes these bright colours seem unsuitable for firemen's uniforms. One unfortunate choice was the yellow chosen for the Royal Exchange Assurance's brigade in 1721, but this was soon changed to a more serviceable pea green. Despite popular belief to the contrary, the different brigades worked closely together and would extinguish all fires in both insured and uninsured property.

During the eighteenth century the tunics were of two types. One was of a simple cut, tight-fitting and worn buttoned up with a belt; the other was of a full cut and worn open with a waistcoat. Breeches were worn by all firemen in the eighteenth century. The uniform of the Foreman (Captain) was similar to that of his men but was distin-guished by a gilt badge and more lace and gold braid.

Although the uniforms look too elaborate for firefighting, there is no firm evidence to suggest that firemen had another working uniform, and civilian clothing at this period was also elaborate and brightly coloured. A new jacket and pair of breeches, later trousers, were issued to the men each year.

Buttons were much in evidence, and probably the greatest number was used by the Phoenix Assurance firemen, who had 56 on their uniforms (twelve on the fall of the jacket, ten on the sleeves, two on the collar, 24 on the waistcoat and eight on the breeches). Early buttons were probably plain, but after the 1750s cast pewter buttons bearing the companies' emblems were used until die-stamped buttons were introduced in the early nineteenth century.

The decorative heading from a late eighteenth-century insurance policy of the Sun Fire Office shows one of their firemen (left) wearing a loose jacket with a full skirt and prominent silver arm badge. His protective helmet is well designed and functional. On the right is a porter (salvage man), employed to remove goods from burning or endangered buildings. He is provided with a jacket but wears his badge on a chain around his neck.

A portrait of George Mead, Foreman (Captain) of the Guardian Assurance Company's fire brigade from 1822 to 1833. He wears a very elaborate uniform of dark brown, decorated with gold braid and many buttons bearing the emblem of the company. His arm badge, which would have been of silver gilt, may be depicted a little larger than it actually was.

Footwear consisted of buckled shoes until the 1740s, when the officers of some brigades were given leather boots. Some of the insurance companies began on a small scale, and their firemen received their uniform piecemeal. For example, the Westminster Insurance Office began in 1717 and provided its twelve firemen with an axe and helmet, but it could not afford to give them a badge and uniform until 1719.

A wide range of materials was used in making the uniforms, the tunic usually being of a hard-wearing woollen material such as kersey cloth, while the breeches were of plush, a strong velvet-like material. Some companies gave their firemen a length of cloth and a sum of money so they could have the uniform individually tailored for a good fit.

The watermen wore a badge on one arm to show they were licensed to operate their boats, and so it was natural that the insurance companies should provide similar badges for their firemen. Initially these were made of sterling silver by a number of famous silversmiths such as Hester Bateman and Thomas Daniell. The badges were beautifully designed and crafted, but costly, and occasionally the men pawned them, although they risked dismissal for doing so. In 1753 the London Assurance Company offered a reward of two guineas (£2.10) for the recovery of a badge lost when the boat of one of its firemen overturned. Around 1810 silver-plated arm or breast badges were worn, and these were superseded by brass badges until eventual replacement by cloth badges.

A very important item of the uniform is the helmet, and although some of the early brigades equipped their men with 'iron caps' the majority of eighteenth-century firemen wore thick leather helmets. These were well designed with raised ribs for additional protection, a pointed peak and a broad protective neckpiece.

About 1800 firemen began wearing a low top hat known as a beaver, despite its apparent unsuitability for fire-fighting. This trend followed a change in naval headwear at this period and was adopted since many of the firemen, who were also Free Watermen, had naval contacts. These hats were worn not only by London brigades, but also by those in Birmingham, Manchester and elsewhere. The beaver evolved into a top hat in some brigades by the 1830s, but some engravings of the period show firemen of the same brigade wearing both types of headwear at fires. However, other brigades had re-adopted helmets by the 1820s, when trousers also began to replace the wearing of breeches.

In 1824 the various insurance brigades in Edinburgh were amalgamated under the command of James Braidwood and given a new standard uniform. This consisted of a short double-breasted tunic, based on the

Above: A silver breast badge, 145 mm high, of a fireman of the West of England Insurance Company, made in 1836 by Philip Venner Firmin. The fireman's number appears on a plinth below King Alfred, the emblem adopted by the company.

Below: A fireman of the Protector Fire Insurance Company (1825-35) wears the top hat favoured by some insurance brigades in the first quarter of the nineteenth century.

design of a naval midshipman's jacket, white canvas trousers and a distinctive leather helmet designed by Braidwood. This uniform was worn by the Edinburgh firemen until replaced with a London Brigade style of tunic around the 1870s.

In 1833 most of the London insurance brigades also amalgamated to form the

Firemen of the Edinburgh Fire Engine Establishment in the 1870s. They wear the distinctive blue tunics and white trousers designed by James Braidwood, their Fire Master (Chief Fire Officer) in 1824. Their leather helmets were painted either yellow, red, blue or grey, corresponding to the four divisions into which the brigade was organised.

London Fire Engine Establishment under the command of James Braidwood, formerly of Edinburgh. He replaced their colourful uniforms with a simpler and more sober one of grey jacket and trousers worn with boots or shoes, and Edinburgh-style leather helmet. With slight variations, this was to remain the London fireman's uniform for the next thirty years.

Some provincial insurance brigades adopted a similar style, while others retained more elaborate types of uniform, but from the 1860s most insurance brigades wore the London Brigade style. The last company brigade was disbanded in 1929. Most volunteer brigades, which began to appear from the 1850s, followed the London style, although industrial brigades wore a variety of uniforms.

Above: A leather fireman's helmet of the style introduced into the London Fire Engine Establishment by James Braidwood in 1833. The epaulettes were recovered from Braidwood's body after he was killed at the Tooley Street fire in 1861.

Below: A fireman of the London Fire Engine Establishment, at the Palace of Westminster fire in 1834, wears the newly introduced uniform designed by James Braidwood, the Superintendent (Chief Fire Officer) of the LFEE. Many brigades adopted (or were adopted by) dogs, which not only became station pets but would accompany them to fires. The dog shown here is Chance, one of the first of these 'fire dogs', who wore a collar engraved 'Stop me not, but onward let me jog, For I am Chance, the London fireman's dog'.

Metal helmets of the type designed by Eyre Massey Shaw. On the left is a silver-plated officer's helmet, made by Merryweather and Sons, bearing the badge of the National Fire Brigades Association. On the right is a brass helmet with the crossed axes badge used by many municipal, volunteer and industrial brigades.

THE FIRE WARRIORS

The eighty years between the 1860s and 1941 was the period of the greatest diversification of brigades in Britain's firefighting history. There existed volunteer, parish, industrial, institutional, country-house, insurance and police-fire brigades, in addition to those maintained by municipal and local authorities.

There was no standardisation of uniforms during this period, and surviving photographs show a large number of variations, not only between brigades but also, in some cases, between men in the same brigade, particularly in the case of volunteers.

There was a gradual trend towards more standardisation in the uniforms worn by volunteer and non-municipal brigades, and this was encouraged by the National Fire Brigades Union from 1887.

In 1911 James Compton Merryweather wrote in *The Fire Brigade Handbook*: 'Running the eye down the ranks at a competition or a procession in which a number of different brigades appeared some twenty years ago, the spectator could not but be struck with the great diversity of appearance amongst those who were taking part in the proceedings. There was the shabby uniform of old fashioned cut, which had manifestly not been renewed for many years. There was the "cheap and nasty", badly-made and of chameleon tints. There was the gaudy cloth of the swell brigade, prominent at fetes and festivals, but of small reputation for firemanship in its native town, and there was the good, substantially well-made uniform, seldom missed amongst the best companies of our working volunteers.'

One of the biggest influences on uniform design occurred in 1866 with the formation of the Metropolitan Fire Brigade in London, which was created to replace the London Fire Engine Establishment which had been maintained by the insurance companies. The Metropolitan firemen were provided with a blue double-breasted tunic and blue trousers made of a stout waterproof cloth, worn with black leather boots and a leather belt. A light but strong brass helmet was designed by the Chief

A fire brigade of the Liverpool and London and Globe Insurance Company at Birstall near Leeds in 1865. In this 'posed action' photograph, the firemen wear leather helmets with a prominent comb and quite long tunics. Trousers have a stripe down each leg, and each man has a pair of gloves tucked into his belt, from which a lifeline is also suspended.

Fire Officer, Eyre Massey Shaw, which was both handsome and practical. The helmet worn by officers was of the same pattern but made of white or 'German' metal, to look like silver.

This basic uniform, with minor variations, was quickly adopted by many brigades around Britain, and worn with either a leather or a brass helmet bearing an appropriate badge. The widespread use of the brass helmet is said to have annoyed Eyre Massey Shaw, who had intended it to have been a distinguishing feature of the Metropolitan Fire Brigade. Brass helmets remained in common use until the 1930s, when the increasing danger of electrocution led to their replacement by non-conducting cork helmets.

Since there was no formal standardisation of uniforms, many brigades would personalise them, a trend most notable among officers. This was easily achieved since manufacturers offered not only vari-

ous basic uniforms for each rank, but also a large range of accessories.

In various parts of Britain police-fire brigades existed: their members carried out normal policing duties but when a fire broke out they took on the role of firemen. Some were provided with firemen's tunics, boots and helmets to wear when attending fires, with perhaps a waterproof coat. The Chief Constable in most cases acted as Chief Fire Officer, and some at the scene of the fire would change their police cap for a leather or brass fireman's helmet.

By the 1880s a wide range of leather helmets was available, besides the ever popular brass. Many were highly ornate, but most were well designed and offered good protection.

Boots, made of grained leather, were offered in two styles: Wellington boots, which reached above the calf but below the knee, with straight tops; and the Napoleon boot, which was cut higher at the front, so

Important Notice.

THIS Catalogue shows a few samples of Firemen's Coats, Helmets, Belts, and other articles of dress. Merryweather & Sons are continually getting out special new designs for home, hot and cold climate use, and invite inspection of such at their Long Acre establishment. Buyers will be enabled thereby to judge that they will get what they require, and at the same time the best value for their money, by going to a first-class house, whose name is a guarantee for the quality.

Fig. 173.
OFFICER IN FULL UNIFORM.

Fig. 174.
FIREMAN IN FULL UNIFORM.

Above: *Illustrations from a maker's catalogue of the 1870s showing Napoleon boots being worn. The officer has an elaborate uniform with braiding on the sleeves. On the front of his tunic is a breast gorget, a decorative metal plate derived from the neckguard of military body armour, and more usually found on soldiers' uniforms. For fire brigade use these gorgets often bear intertwined initials and crossed axes.*

providing protection for the knee. Rubber boots first appeared in the 1900s but were not widely adopted until the 1930s.

Various waterproof mackintoshes were available from at least the 1890s, but there is little evidence to show how widely they were used by the fire brigades.

Buttons were usually in silvered metal for officers and of brass for the firemen, and they might be of a stock pattern, the most popular types of which were a helmet with crossed axes or the insignia of the National Fire Brigades Union (from 1919 known as the National Fire Brigades Association). Municipal and volunteer brigades had coats of arms, titles or entwined

Right: *A fireman of Southend-on-Sea Fire Brigade in 1907 wears a double-breasted tunic with turned-down collar and fold-back sleeves. His leather helmet is a 'Number 2 Volunteer' pattern. Around his neck he wears what appears to be a neckerchief.*

11

Eston Urban District Fire Brigade, Cleveland, in 1922. The Chief Fire Officer holds a dog, while on his left is the Brigade Captain, distinguished by a pair of double epaulettes, and on his right is the Second Officer with one double epaulette. The firemen wear their London Brigade pattern undress caps and hold their brass helmets. Tunics are also of the widely adopted London Brigade pattern.

Darlaston Fire Brigade, West Midlands, c.1900. They wear a military style of undress uniform, that of the Captain (centre) being particularly elaborate. All the members of the brigade wear whistles (except for the officer on the far right), with the sockets attached to their belts. The man seated second from the left may be the engineer; note his cap.

A selection of tunic buttons from volunteer or non-municipal fire brigades: (from left to right, top row), Phoenix Fire Office, c.1810; Sun Fire Office, c.1840s; County Fire Office, c.1860s; (second row) Hilton Castle Fire Brigade; Sutton Volunteer Fire Brigade; Hastings and St Leonards Volunteer Fire Brigade; (third row) Co-operative Wholesale Society Fire Brigade; National Fire Brigades Union button, pre-1919; National Fire Brigades Association button, post-1919; (fourth row) General Volunteer pattern; Vickers Armstrong Fire Brigade; Royal Ordnance Factory Fire Brigade.

initials on their buttons, while insurance brigades used the companies' emblems.

In some brigades where the firemen all wore leather helmets, the Captain was supplied with a brass or silver one, but the usual distinguishing features for officers were metal epaulettes made of overlapping scales. These were made of brass, chromed brass or white metal, but because of the lack of standardisation there were variations in both style and use. While some brigades used chromed epaulettes for the Chief Fire Officer and brass double epaulettes for the Second and Third Officers, others had double epaulettes only for the Chief Officer and used single epaulettes for the Sub-officers; these were worn in pairs. Engineers in some brigades wore a single epaulette, while all the members of Aberystwyth Fire Brigade in the 1890s wore a pair of double epaulettes, with the Captain distinguished by wearing a cap and a whistle, and the Second Officer by sergeant's stripes.

The Metropolitan Fire Brigade also had an influence on the undress uniform of various brigades, worn when engaged in duties about the fire station or on stand-by. Many of the London firemen and their officers, including some of the Chief Fire Officers, were ex-navy men, who would have been familiar with the similar duty

systems operated by both the Royal Navy and the London Fire Brigade. This established a tradition which persisted from the 1840s until the Second World War.

The naval influence showed itself most clearly in the firemen's headwear worn with undress uniform, which was a brimless cap whose badge or ribbon wore the brigade's name. This cap, known as the London Brigade pattern, was adopted by the majority of British brigades, although a few favoured a military-style peaked cap, and some a form of forage cap. Sheffield Fire Brigade around 1890 carried the naval influence even further by providing its men not only with a naval-style cap but also with a sailor's tunic, complete with navy neck and lanyard.

In some brigades the working tunic was worn as part of the undress uniform, but many had a lighter serge tunic or jacket. These jackets appear in a variety of different styles, but it is in the undress uniform of officers that the greatest variation in design, style and embellishment can be seen. Other brigade personnel might also wear distinctive undress uniforms or badges, particularly drivers, engineers and brigade doctors.

In general there seems to have been a leaning towards either a naval style of dress for officers and men or a military-based

Medals were worn on formal occasions. Some officers had won many decorations, and Superintendent La Croix of Brighton Fire Brigade was photographed in the 1920s wearing his numerous medals. His jacket is of the naval style worn by many officers up to 1939.

style. This was probably determined in many cases by the preference (and experience) of either the Chief Fire Officer, the Captain or the fire brigade committee, but local variations made each brigade different in some respect from all the others.

Uniform manufacturers produced medals in a wide variety of designs for use by fire brigades. These were presented to the firemen for long service or acts of bravery, and to the winners of competitions. The Society for the Protection of Life from Fire, founded in 1843, also issued awards for acts of bravery. Medals came complete with a ribbon in a velvet-lined box and were intended to be worn on parades and other special occasions, never while firefighting.

From the 1890s the National Fire Brigades Union (later Association) issued long-service medals in bronze and silver, with the length of service shown on a bar attached to the ribbon. These were used by many brigades and have the recipient's name, brigade (sometimes only its initials) and date of issue engraved on it. The London County Council, when it took over the London Fire Brigade in 1889, issued its own long-service medals.

FIG. 1110

OFFICERS' PARADE CAP.

Above: *The obverse and reverse of a medal issued by the Society for the Protection of Life from Fire to Captain Henry Eydmann, Captain of the Chiswick Volunteer Fire Brigade, in 1905. In January of that year Captain Eydmann rescued two women from a burning house, carrying them down a ladder, despite the fact that he was then 57 years old and the oldest member of Chiswick Fire Brigade.*

Below: *Not all helmets were made of leather or brass, and this example is made of moulded felt. This was the cheapest type of helmet available, although this example has a number of ornaments which would have made it a little more expensive.*

FIG. 1111.

Above: *Some Captains and Chief Officers favoured a wide frogging on their undress uniform, following a style used by some army regiments for officers' undress wear. In this example the officer is shown with a kepi-style cap. Above is shown an officers' parade cap, although this style was not very common.*

15

Firemen relax at a National Fire Brigades Association training camp in the 1920s. It is unusual to find photographs of this period showing what the men wore under their tunics. All wear London Brigade pattern undress caps, some wear waistcoats, and most wear shirts with separate collars and ties, although the seated man, drinking, appears to have a dicky front with winged collar.

Now fire brigades issue the Royal Warrant Queen's Long Service Medal, while outstanding acts of bravery are recognised by the award of the British Empire Medal, George Cross or George Medal.

The First World War affected the fire brigades as members resigned to join the army for a war expected to last only six months or so, and later as reservists were called up.

Although bombs were dropped on England, killing a total of 1413 people between December 1914 and March 1918 and starting a considerable number of fires, no special adaptations were made to the fireman's uniform.

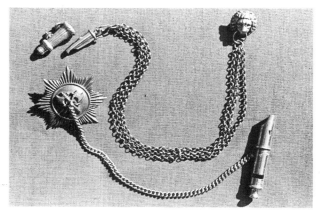

Whistles were used by officers to give commands and warnings, and they were often ornate with elaborate attachment plates. The upper example has the whistle fitted into a chased socket which was attached to the tunic or belt. Below is a double-ended signalling whistle which produces two tones, so increasing the number of commands that could be given.

16

Bainbridges Department Store, Newcastle upon Tyne, had a private fire brigade drawn from volunteers among the staff. When the men were called up for military service in the First World War their place in the brigade was taken by these apprentices, lady shop assistants and staff too young or too old for wartime service. However, only the men got firemen's tunics. To the right is Station Officer Nicholson of the City Fire Brigade, who inspected the store brigade every six months.

A fireman of the Auxiliary Fire Service (left) in his working uniform of tunic, oilskin overtrousers and rubber boots. Being a member of the London AFS, he has a hose spanner suspended from his belt as well as an axe. The firewoman (right) is wearing one of about twenty variations of uniform for female personnel issued during the war. However, they were expected to supply their own stockings, which had to be of lisle and a 'maple shade'.

The problem of the Auxiliary fireman only having one uniform was graphically expressed in a cartoon by Ben Betts, himself an Auxiliary fireman, which was published in 1941.

'HEROES WITH GRIMY FACES'

By 1935 the British government had begun to see the possibility of another war in Europe and issued an Air Raid Precautions Circular to all local authorities. However, this included almost no mention of firefighting, and it was not until 1937 that the Home Office issued a circular entitled 'Emergency Fire Brigade Organisation' which asked the many fire authorities to submit proposals on the recruiting and training of auxiliary firemen, the establishment of auxiliary fire stations, and the improvement of water supplies. The same year the London Fire Brigade replaced the traditional brass helmet with a cork one.

In 1938 a draft bill was passed by Parliament which was intended to improve the standards, efficiency and organisation of Britain's various types of fire brigades, and recruitment of personnel into the Auxiliary Fire Service (AFS) began. This went slowly at first, but by March 1939 some 140,000 people had volunteered. The government estimated that 350,000 would be needed in the event of war.

Although there were a few women's fire brigades in the Victorian and Edwardian period and women had joined industrial brigades during the First World War, it was the first time that women had been recruited into the mainstream fire service. They carried out such varied duties as communications, dispatch riding and driving, but for the first year or two some were involved in firefighting.

It became obvious that the traditional style of a fireman's helmet could not be produced in large enough numbers to supply the needs of the AFS, and among the headwear considered for wartime use by firemen was a military-style steel helmet. This was adopted for all firemen, although with considerable hesitation since brass helmets had only just been phased out because of the increasing danger of electrocution. Steel helmets were chosen because before the war the use of blister gas had been feared and it was pointed out that steel helmets could be boiled, unlike those made of leather or cork.

A number of firemen received electric shocks through their steel helmets, but the first fatality, when Column Officer Joseph Entwistle was electrocuted in 1942, led to calls for a safer alternative, particularly the compressed leather helmet worn by workers in explosives factories. These were not, however, accepted and firemen continued to wear the steel 'battle-bowler' until the end of the war, and even later.

The AFS firemen were initially provided with a peaked cap, overalls, rubber boots and a grey steel helmet, while Officers wore a white helmet with varying red bands indicating their rank. In London all ranks also had a hose spanner worn in a special pouch

Left: *A fireman of the Auxiliary Fire Service wears a dark blue overall with a canvas belt. Several variations in the pattern of overalls existed, and boots were often worn on duty and when firefighting. The peaked cap was provided as undress wear.*

Right: *Fireman A. Phillips of C Company, National Fire Service Overseas Contingent. He wears the distinctive beret of these firemen, who underwent training to accompany the British forces landing in Europe.*

on their belt since the London Fire Brigade did not adopt the instantaneous coupling until several months into the war. Later that year the issue of a tunic, trousers and waterproof leggings was authorised, but they received only one set each, and there was no overcoat.

Friction existed between the AFS and the regular brigade on a number of points, including the fact that the regulars had two working uniforms, so they always had a dry one available. The AFS personnel were forced to continue to wear their wet uniforms, although back at their stations many would have to clean equipment in their underclothes while their uniforms dried out. The AFS appealed to the government for a second set, but it was turned down on the grounds of cost. However, some AFS

men were given regular firemen's uniforms when they replaced regular firemen who were drafted into the army. In November 1940 the government finally agreed to give the AFS a second uniform, but it was some months before the men received them, and by then they had been involved in almost continuous firefighting for many weeks.

To improve efficiency and prevent continuing friction it was decided to nationalise the fire brigades for the duration of the war, and the National Fire Service (NFS) came into existence in 1941. A standardised uniform was introduced, which for ranks below Company Officer consisted of a fire tunic which was worn on all occasions, while officers had a dark blue undress uniform and a fire tunic with rank markings on the shoulder straps. Since over a hundred thousand AFS tunics had already been issued it was decided to accept this pattern as standard, as well as the AFS peaked cap which replaced the London Brigade pattern cap worn by many members of the fire service for over eighty years.

The NFS had a new rank system, including five female officer grades. Officers were distinguished by wearing metal 'pips' whose design was based on the impeller of a pump, on shoulder straps which replaced the traditional scale epaulettes. The size and number indicated rank, Divisional Officers and above having the addition of a laurel wreath. A similar system of rank markings is still used by the fire brigade today, although the impeller design has been further stylised.

Firemen and firewomen clerks were distinguished by a white metal letter A worn on the lapel of their tunics, while back-up staff such as mechanics, fitters and maintenance staff were also given a uniform.

Dispatch riders were provided with a blue battledress instead of a tunic.

In 1943 volunteers were requested from the ranks of the NFS to accompany the proposed invasion fleet to Europe, and more men than required came forward. Their function was to protect equipment and ammunition dumps on the beach-head with fire appliances of various types and a number of fireboats. Four columns, each of five hundred men, were formed and supplied with a modified uniform consisting of a blue beret in place of a peaked cap, a red shoulder flash marked 'Overseas Contingent', a khaki webbing belt instead of a blue one, and army boots and khaki anklets. They underwent special training and were placed on stand-by. However, the army invited men of Section Leader rank or above to apply for a commission in the Pioneer Corps, a unit of which formed the Army Fire Service, in January 1944. This unit was then deployed in the D-Day

An inspection of National Fire Service members illustrates the uniforms of a number of different ranks, the officers' tunics being based on a military pattern. (Facing camera, left to right) Company Officer, Chief Regional Fire Officer and Divisional Officer. (Back to camera, centre) Leading Fireman. (To his right) A dispatch rider, who wears a blouse.

RANK	SHOULDER MARKINGS (BOTH SHOULDERS)	STEEL HELMET
Chief Regional Fire Officer		
Fire Force Commander		
Assistant Fire Force Commander		
Divisional Officer		
Column Officer		
Senior Company Officer		
Company Officer		
Section Leader		
Leading Fireman		
Fireman		

The shoulder and steel-helmet markings used by the National Fire Service from its inception in 1941.

landings in June instead of the Overseas Contingent.

In October 1944 three of the four columns were demobilised, but the fourth continued training for emergency use. Their chance came in January 1945 when they were allocated to the Advanced Sections Communication Zone of the United States Army in Europe and performed firefighting duties in various parts of France and Germany. The firemen in the forward areas replaced their blue tunics and trousers with United States khaki denim, although they still retained the status of 'persons accompanying armed forces'.

The firefighters became national heroes during the Blitz, a reputation they were to maintain, and Winston Churchill referred to the firemen as 'the heroes with grimy faces'. During the war many members of the fire brigade won awards for bravery and distinguished service, but 793 firemen and 25 firewomen were killed on duty, and over seven thousand were injured.

'Control Room in Action', painted by Reginald Mills in 1943. National Fire Service firewomen are operating a switchboard and telephones, while another is using an operational board mounted on the wall. Two Company Officers, distinguished by a broad red stripe on their helmets, are also present.

Firemen of Tynemouth Fire Brigade on parade in the mid 1960s. The firemen are wearing black cork helmets with a solid cork comb, a style worn by most brigades at this time. However, in this case they incorporate an unusual feature, since they have a fitting on the comb to which a miner's lamp can be fitted. Axes and lifelines were worn by firemen until the late 1970s.

A GOOD UNIFORM MUST WORK

When the brigades were nationalised in 1941 the government gave an undertaking that they would return to local authority control when hostilities ceased. It was tentatively suggested that the National Fire Service should remain in place, but this was opposed by the local authorities, and on 1st April 1948 the fire brigades were denationalised. They now came under the control of 140 fire authorities, which replaced the 1440 of pre-war days.

However, government control was still exercised in many aspects, including the standardisation of the uniforms. Chief Officers or fire brigade committees were no longer able to design their own style of uniform for their men, and the embellish-

ments favoured by some Chief Officers were no longer allowed.

A number of styles of uniforms and helmets for the new brigades were considered and tested, but tunics of melton material, of the same design as those worn by National Fire Service firemen, were specified, while epaulettes were reintroduced for officers. Steel helmets were replaced by cork helmets of the traditional design, soon followed by those of phenolic resin and other new materials. Leather was once again used in place of rubber for boots.

Local authorities were allowed to distinguish their brigade uniforms by using buttons incorporating their coat of arms or other devices, while badges on helmets and

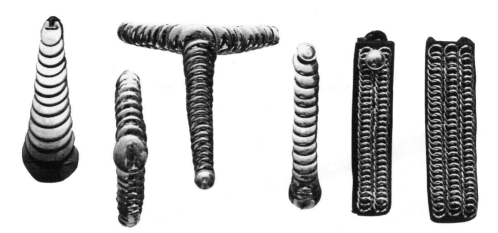

Above: *For many years shoulder epaulettes were worn to indicate rank. This system was suspended during the Second World War but resumed again in 1948 with slightly smaller, chromed epaulettes. These were used until the 1960s, when replaced by a system of rank markings similar to those used by the National Fire Service. (Far left) Pre-war, brass, single scale epaulette. All the others are 1949 pattern, chromed: (left to right) Station Officer, Divisional Officer, Assistant Divisional Officer, Deputy Chief Officer and Chief Officer.*

Below right: *A selection of tunic buttons of municipal brigades. (From left to right: top row) Stoke-on-Trent, brass, 1920s; City of Edinburgh, brass, pre-1941; Brighton Fire Brigade, brass, pre-1941. (Second row) Cheltenham, brass, pre-1941; Edinburgh, nickel, 1948/9; National Fire Service, nickel, 1941-8. (Third row) Leeds, chrome, 1947-74; London, chrome, 1965; Cheshire, chrome, 1974. (Fourth row) Tyne and Wear, chrome, 1974; Nottinghamshire, chrome, 1979; South Yorkshire, chrome, 1974.*

caps were placed on an eight-pointed star.

Initially undress uniform for firemen seems to have been in short supply and some were provided with a navy-blue battledress (like National Fire Service dispatch riders), a peaked cap and army ammunition boots, although there appear to have been wide variations between brigades. Officers wore the same type of undress uniform as in the National Fire Service, which was based on the undress uniform of infantry officers.

Later the firemen were issued with a high-necked jacket of pre-war style, and later still an open-necked undress jacket of serge, available in several styles, which was worn with a collar and tie. Rank badges for undress uniform were similar to those of the National Fire Service.

The political situation in Europe began to deteriorate into the Cold War, and the gov-

25

Firewomen's uniform of the 1960s. The jacket style had been used for many years, although the skirt was shortened to conform to the fashionable length of the period.

ernment felt it prudent to reconstitute the Auxiliary Fire Service and Civil Defence Corps. Recruiting began in 1949, and it was hoped to recruit fifty thousand auxiliary firemen and five thousand firewomen. However, by 1955 only fifteen thousand people had joined. They were better uniformed than their pre-war predecessors, and, although what they were issued with did vary from area to area, most seem to have had a cap, steel helmet, two tunics and two pairs of trousers, battledress, working overalls, boots and shoes, while many, if not all, were provided with the helmets

worn by brigades in their area. The Auxiliary Fire Service was disbanded in 1968.

In the 1950s the Cornish branch of the National Association of Fire Officers suggested that a reefer jacket, with naval-style rank markings on the sleeves, should be introduced for officers, but this idea was not well received and it came to nothing.

By the 1960s the job of a fireman had diversified, with fires involving a greater range of materials and chemicals, and with increasing attendance at such incidents as road traffic accidents, and there was a feeling that uniform design could be improved to cope with and protect the wearer from a wide range of hazards.

In the mid 1960s a new Du Pont fibre, known as Nomex, was used for firemen's tunics in the United States of America, and in 1970 trials of Nomex tunics were begun in Britain by the Uniform Committee of the Central Fire Brigades Advisory Council (CFBAC). The same considerations applied to uniforms in the 1970s as in the 1870s: they should be comfortable for the wearer, allow perspiration to evaporate and air to circulate to keep the wearer cool, should protect the body from heat, be waterproof and look smart. The tests proved Nomex a good material for tunics as it fulfilled the committee's requirements. In 1974 it was recommended as the material ideally suited for firemen's uniforms, and over the next decade it became widely used for tunics and trousers.

A steel helmet with transfer badge of the type authorised by the Home Office for use by county and county borough fire brigades in the 1970s. This style of helmet was not very popular.

The 1970s were a period of experimentation with different types of uniform, one of the more unusual being a battery-powered heated tunic lining for use in conditions of extreme cold, but it was not a success. Overtrousers or leggings, formerly always black, became yellow, while rubber boots were once again used by some brigades, although others continued with improved designs of leather boots.

In 1975 officers in Warwickshire began wearing a naval-style pullover in place of tunics on less formal occasions, and in 1979 the CFBAC suggested that these be introduced for all ranks. In the mid 1970s the CFBAC recommended that firemen's helmets should be painted canary yellow, in place of black, with those of officers painted white with black rank bands.

Changes were also made to the style of working rig worn when on duties about the fire station.

In the 1980s the Nomex tunics were made longer, and gaberdine raincoats began to be replaced by anoraks. Waistcoat-style reflective jackets, worn at road traffic accidents, were superseded in some brigades by full overjackets with reflective strips, and these strips also appeared on tunics, with increasing use of Velcro fasteners. The uniforms worn by female personnel were also modernised in the mid 1980s, while in the late 1980s some brigades introduced a more civilian style of undress uniform jacket for firemen, although still worn with a peaked cap.

The fireman's uniform is still undergoing change to meet the new hazards and con-

Firemen's uniform was increasingly streamlined in the 1980s, with widespread use of new materials. Safety features included reflective strips and a prominent badge bearing the word 'Fire'.

Left: *In the 1980s the undress uniform of firemen was changed from a double-breasted tunic, with no breast pocket, to a jacket based on an officer's style. At the same time the uniform of female personnel was also changed to a jacket based on the officer style, worn with an 'A-line' skirt and a hat like that already being worn by control officers. A shoulder bag was supplied as part of the uniform.*

Right: *In 1990 the London Fire Brigade began to introduce helmets with a visor for additional protection. With the increasing chances of encountering toxic gases at a fire, the wearing of breathing apparatus has become more common, leading to improved lightweight equipment.*

ditions encountered by modern fire brigades, notably in the adoption of new helmets and longer tunics, and it has been suggested that a one-piece working suit may be finally chosen, with a more traditional style of uniform supplied for formal occasions. Now, three hundred years after the fireman's uniform was introduced to Britain, its design will be determined by considerations for the comfort and safety of the wearer rather than the dictates of fashion.

An atmospheric smoke hood of 1843. Fresh air is pumped to the wearer from a foot bellows outside the building, an idea put forward in 1830, and passes down a tube into the jacket, which is tightly belted at waist and cuffs. Stale air is expelled through a one-way valve in the face mask.

CLAD IN ARMOUR

During the eighteenth century it was realised that a fire could be more efficiently extinguished if hose could be taken inside the building to the seat of the fire. Rescuing people often required the firemen to enter a burning building, but smoke, poisonous gases, heat or lack of oxygen would drive the rescuers out and, on occasion, kill them. Therefore much thought was given to developing protective devices.

The earliest type used a hood with a tube attached, the end of which was placed in fresh air, and the wearers relied on lung power to draw air down the tube, but breathing was not easy, particularly during exertion. An improvement on this was the addition of a bellows to the end of the tube to pump fresh air to the fireman, who wore a hooded overjacket. More recent examples consisted of a smoke mask, without

overjacket, connected to the bellows, and in some brigades these were available until the late 1940s or early 1950s. All these atmospheric types had the big drawback of being cumbersome, since the wearer had to uncoil the air tube as he moved forward and lay it out behind him. Retreat had to be along the route of the air line, so if that way became blocked the wearer was trapped.

These difficulties provided a strong incentive to develop a self-contained breathing apparatus which would eliminate the need for the air tube. The first modern respirator was devised in 1875 by Professor Tyndall and Eyre Massey Shaw and drew air through a canister containing various filtering elements.

Although respirators would filter out smoke and some gases, it was some time before it was realised that one of the great-

est dangers when entering a burning building came from a lack of oxygen, and the only way to overcome this was to carry an air supply. An apparatus with a self-contained supply of oxygen was produced for use in mines in 1881, but not adopted by many fire brigades until after the First World War. In 1919 large fires in Newcastle and Birmingham caused many fatalities, including two firemen. It was realised that more people could have been saved if self-contained breathing apparatus had been available. As a result a variety of self-contained apparatus was produced and in turn improved, resulting in the development of today's well designed, lightweight and reliable equipment.

To allow a closer approach to the fire in order to control it more effectively, fire-resistant suits made of woven asbestos fibre came into use in the 1920s. The Second World War created a much wider demand for asbestos suits, hoods, gloves and aprons.

After the war fire-resistant suits of aluminised asbestos were used mainly by

Above: While often described as an eighteenth-century smoke mask, this closely resembles a Roberts Hood Respirator of the 1840s. This had a trumpet-shaped pipe, 2 feet (61 cm) long, attached to the nosepiece of the mask and secured to the uniform buttons by straps to stop it swinging. In the bottom of the tube was a sponge soaked in water.

Right: Resembling a deep-sea diver's helmet, this atmospheric smoke hood, worn over the tunic, dates to the 1920s. Such equipment, which included a lifeline and a manually operated air pump, came in a strong wooden box with the instructions inside the lid.

30

Royal Air Force, airport and some industrial brigades, but more recently the dangers to health of asbestos fibres have been realised. Close-proximity firefighting suits are now available in such materials as aluminised rayon and aluminised carbon fibre, with hoods of a flame-retardant shell with epoxy-coated aluminium finish.

Increasingly modern fire brigades attend incidents involving chemical hazards. The origin of the fireman's chemical suit can be found in the anti-gas protective clothing issued to brigades during the Second World War, but fortunately never required. Today's chemical suits consist of flexible PVC or a polyester material with various coatings.

Right: *King George VI examines regenerative breathing apparatus during an inspection of the London Fire Brigade. Oxygen from the cylinder on the fireman's back is gradually fed into the system, but the wearer's exhaled air goes into a breathing bag on the chest. It is then chemically purified to remove carbon dioxide before being reinhaled. The apparatus could be used for one hour.*

FURTHER READING

Little has been published specifically about the development of the fireman's uniform, and the books listed below deal with a particular aspect of the uniform, give a good outline of fire brigade history, or include plenty of photographs of different types of uniform.

Akers, M. A. *British Fire Service Cap Badges 1974-85. Volume I.* Published by author, 1985 (ISBN 0 9510 932 0 7).
Akers, M. A. *British Fire Service Cap Badges 1947-74. Volume II.* Published by author, 1989 (ISBN 0 9510 932 1 5).
Bain, F., and Wright, B. *Fire Insurance Company Buttons.* The Fire Mark Circle, 1985.
Blackstone, G. V. A. *A History of the British Fire Service.* Routledge and Kegan Paul, 1957.
Creighton, J. *Firefighting in Action.* Blandford Press, 1985.
Cunnington, P., and Lucas, C. *Occupational Costume in England.* Adam and Charles Black, 1967.
Ewing, E. *Women in Uniform through the Centuries.* B. T. Batsford, 1975.
Green-Hughes, E. *A History of Firefighting.* Moorland Publishing, 1979.
Henham, B., and Sharp, B. *Badges of Extinction. The 18th and 19th Century Badges of Insurance Firemen.* Quiller Press, 1989.
Ingram, A. *A History of Fire Fighting and Equipment.* New English Library, 1978.
de Lasa, C. *Firemen to the Rescue.* Moonlight Publishing, 1987.
Paul, T. *The Story of the Fire Service.* Almark Publishing, 1975.
Rickards, M. *The World Fights Fire.* Longman, 1971.

Vince, J. *Fire-marks*. Shire Publications, 1973.
Wallington, N. *Firemen at War*. David and Charles, 1981.
Wright, B. *Firefighting Equipment*. Shire Publications, 1989.

PLACES TO VISIT

Some city, county and local museums have on display or in their collections items of firemen's uniform, usually from a local brigade. Examples of some of the many different types of uniform can be seen in collections held by some fire brigades, which can be viewed by appointment. Uniforms and other items can be seen at the following museums. Intending visitors are advised to find out the opening times before making a special journey.

Horsham Museum, Causeway House, 9 The Causeway, Horsham, West Sussex RH12 1HE. Telephone: 0403 54959.

Museum of Fire, Lothian and Borders Fire Brigade Headquarters, Lauriston Place, Edinburgh EH3 9DE. Telephone: 031-228 2401.

South Yorkshire Fire Service Museum, 101-9 West Bar, Sheffield, South Yorkshire. Telephone: 0742 752147.

Fireproof suits of aluminised asbestos are particularly suitable for use by brigades dealing with aircraft crashes, since a close approach to the fire can be made. Here a fireman pours foam on to an aeroplane fire.